Memories *of the* Great American Ice Shows

by

JIMMY LAWRENCE

CREDITS

I want to thank those who have provided special help and information and also list books given, owned, or loaned that have proven to be informative. If I have failed to recognize you and you have helped, please forgive me. I am an amateur, and this is a work of the heart. Here are some of those folks who have steered me in one direction or another.

CONTRIBUTORS:

Tom Collins, Helen Maxson, Marshall Beard, Sid Spaulding, and George Shipstad

SUPPORT:

Judith Allen, Amy Pulitzer, Robin Reid, Jeannette Brinker, David Brinker and Michael Burgess.

SPECIAL ACKNOWLEDGEMENT:

Thanks to my dear wife Lenora for her invaluable technical and editing support and her help and encouragement.

To all those talented people who made the great American ice shows possible and to the many outstanding professionals with whom I was privileged to share the ice.

Preface

During my years as a principal performer with both Ice Capades and Holiday on Ice, I was privileged to know most of the people associated with the birth of the major touring ice shows. The nature of the business tended to create an exclusive community, and we knew each other as most folks know the close and extended members of their own families. This family was a microcosm of the rest of the country at a special time in the history of our country and of the touring great American ice shows.

In 2000 an Ice Capades reunion was held in Las Vegas, and, although I had been away from the business for nearly fifty years and had created another life, that still small voice that sometimes speaks to us urged me to go. Over seven hundred attended. The majority were not of my era, but twenty or so of my vintage managed to find each other that night and all of us, though changed by time, were delighted to see one another and eager to share our life experiences since the last curtain call. The old feeling was still there, and we were still family.

Reminiscing with the group over cocktails that evening, I realized that we were the remnant of a great and rare part of entertainment history. Others have written about the founding of the shows and the history of ice-skating, but I know of no book that includes personal memories of what it was like to have been a participant in those phenomenal early shows. This book introduces you to the founders and some early performers, provides glimpses into day-to-day life in a touring company, and relates some backstage anecdotes about the early touring shows.

Memories of Great American Ice Shows will provide you with a bit of insight into the wonder and spectacle of the early touring ice shows.

Ice Shows – The Inception

Once upon a time, not that long ago, a glamorous and enchanting new form of entertainment rose up and took our country by storm. The great American ice shows were phenomenal extravaganzas the likes of which had never before been seen. They toured the country bringing quality entertainment to the average citizen—large ensembles with fine skaters, fantastic sets, glamorous gals, handsome guys, dazzling costumes, live orchestras, clowns, comedians, and hilarious novelty acts! Technicians skilled in the art of special effects used the latest advancements in sound and light technology to enhance the magic and glamor of each number. The shows came to your hometown—or within driving distance—with an entertainment package for every member of the family. The lights came on and the spectacle of dozens of skaters in elegant costumes surrounded by spectacular sets would cause the audience to gasp out loud in delight.

Those early shows served as a valuable morale booster and brief respite for a country totally engaged in a terrible global war, World War II. They were immensely popular with audiences of all ages, and in their heyday, they grossed more money than major league baseball.

The environment and timing has to be just right for a new entity to survive. In the early thirties, the United States was fertile ground in which these new concepts could grow and flourish.

Perhaps ice shows had their birth in Russia where citizens combined their love of ballet and skating, transferring it to ice. In 1915, interest in ice dancing surged when a young German girl, Charlotte Oelschlägel, came to New York City to perform the first ballet on ice in the Hippodrome. Ice shows were also becoming popular in Bournemouth, Manchester, Brighton, and Richmond, England. Many stars, who would later appear in the great American touring shows, performed in those outdoor shows in the twenties and early thirties including Nate Walley, Orin Markhus, Evelyn Chandler, Robert Dench and Rosemarie Stewart, Eric Waite, Red McCarthy, Viviane Hulten, and Freddie Trenkler.

Figure skating emerged and flourished in Europe where skating on lakes, ponds, and rivers was a common pastime in the cold winter months. The first blades were smoothed bones that enabled the skater to move speedily across the ice. Later ten- or twelve-inch pieces of sharpened metal were fashioned and attached by straps to winter footwear. When skaters began to attempt ballet-like maneuvers on ice, the figure skate blade became shorter and curved at the front. An evolutionary leap occurred when skaters discovered toe picks. With picks fashioned on the curved surface at the front of the blade, they could speed backward, place the picks from one foot into the ice, use their speed to propel their bodies into the air, spin, and continue in a forward direction.

Early European skaters enjoyed tracing complex figures on outdoor frozen rinks. A favorite figure in those days was a "heart on one leg," which became known as a three turn. Then a few in their ranks began to attempt various leaps, jumps, and spins similar to those seen in ballet. Ulrich Salchow and Axel Paulsen of Sweden brought these developing skills to the United States and Canada. At the same time, elite figure skating clubs formed in key cities in both countries.

Competitions followed, but it was definitely the sport of the wealthy. The early competitions centered on the skaters' ability to do intricate tracings on the ice, known as "school figures," which counted for 60 percent of the score. Ballet moves, called free skating, counted 40 percent. As a result, in the twenties and thirties, the champions were not exciting to watch, and few were hired by the early ice shows. Robin Lee was an exception. Five-time US Senior Men's Champion from St. Paul, Minnesota, Robin came from humble means. His father, A. R. Lee, taught figure skating and trained Robin.

Those who couldn't afford the clubs, the blue and gray collar crowd in the eastern and midwestern United States and in the east and central Canada, took streetcars or walked to frozen lakes, rivers, and ponds. Entertainment during that era consisted of Nickelodeons, concerts in the park, Vaudeville, touring companies of great Broadway shows, and local amateur and professional presentations. These skaters attempted to duplicate things they had seen on the stage and performed everything from dance to comedy before crowds that would gather along the banks of the frozen rivers, lakes, and ponds.

It was these self-taught, blue collar skaters who would populate the early ice shows. Though often self-taught, they were highly skilled in free skating and had great audience appeal. As ice shows matured and the scoring system for the competitions changed to 50 percent figures, 50 percent free skating, good free skaters moved to the fore and were hired by the major shows. Some of the early elite champions may have viewed making a living performing in any ice show as a bit demeaning; however, a number of them, including Maribel Vinson and Viviane Hulten, became excellent instructors.

Petite Sonja Henie of Norway had won Olympic Gold Medals in 1928, 1932, and 1936. Sweden's Viviane Hulten was a great amateur champion, as were Heidi Stenof of Austria and Maribell Vinson of the United States. As featured events of winter carnivals in the Midwest, the Shipstad brothers and Oscar Johnson were wowing crowds, bundled up at outdoor ice rinks. In the East and across Canada, the exclusive private skating clubs put on amateur ice reviews that featured the Scandinavians, Ulrich Salchow, Axel Paulsen, or the American, Jackson Haines, who were each rapidly expanding what could be done on figure skates.

The elements were falling into place for the birth of one of the one of the most unique and spectacular entertainment mediums of all time.

The era of the magnificent, glamorous touring extravaganzas bloomed and flourished, then passed into history and will never be seen again, and I was fortunate to have been a part of that world. Here is my story.

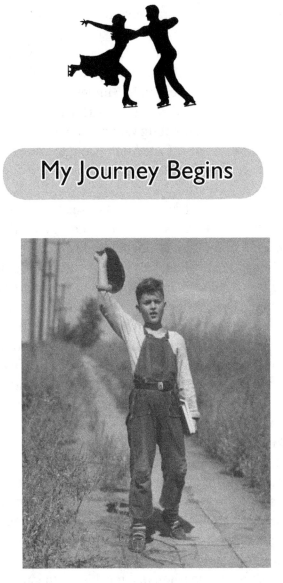

My Journey Begins

1. Jamie Lawrence, St. Paul, Minnesota, Age 9

Lying on my bed when I was about four years old, I had just received an adrenaline shot to relieve a severe asthma attack. My mother, father, and a doctor stood beside my bed. My dear mother had tears in her eyes and was clearly distraught, my father stoic. The doctor, stethoscope around his neck, had just told my parents, "I don't think he's going to make it this time."

That was my first memory of life with asthma. The scene with the doctor would be repeated several more times, and the doctor would also repeat the prediction that I wouldn't make it.

As a child, I would sit on my screened-in front porch watching the other children play during the summer and early fall. I couldn't join them during the pollination season in Minnesota for fear of bringing on an attack. That changed one day when I was ten years old. My dad took me downtown for my first hot fudge sundae at the St. Paul Hotel. On the way, we dropped into the St. Paul Auditorium to watch the figure skaters. At the time, the St. Paul Auditorium was one of the few places in the country with indoor artificial ice, and the world's top figure skaters flocked there to work out. I was excited to see these greats performing and amazed at their skill. Even more astounding, my asthma had vanished! The moist ice rink environment eliminated the pollens in the air.

To my delight, Dad decided that I should take up figure skating, and our next stop was Kennedy Brothers Arms, the finest sporting goods store in the state. Dad believed the cheapest investment in anything was to buy the best, so I was promptly outfitted with a pair of CCM (Canadian Cycle Motors) boots and blades. CCM were best known as the premiere maker of hockey skates and equipment. I was proud of my new skates as I ventured forth with what I thought was the best. I couldn't imagine such things as custom-fitted boots or handmade blades. With those store-bought skates I won the Midwestern Championship, gained national ranking, and became the male lead in Ice Capades.

Like all Minnesota boys, I played hockey during the winter for a number of years, but figure skating was a new experience. I had always been a little small for hockey and was often knocked around. Figure skating seemed to come naturally to me. My family couldn't afford an extensive lesson program, but I did have a few, and by closely observing the nation's and world's best, I was able to learn quite a bit. Later, I worked as a bus boy in a teashop in a local department store earning the magnificent sum of thirty-one cents an hour and was able to contribute toward a few more lessons.

In 1941 at the age of fourteen, I passed the required skating tests and qualified to compete in the Junior Midwestern Championships in Chicago. My family couldn't afford to go to the competitions with me and sent me off to Chicago by myself. Much to my delight, I learned I would be traveling on the shiny new Burlington Zephyr Streamliner, the first diesel-electric passenger train in the country. The Zephyrs were promoted as "the last word in passenger service."

It had set a speed record, averaging a breath-taking seventy-seven miles per hour. Unlike the other streamliners, it was stainless steel and utilized a new welding process rather than bolts, which gave it a sleek, futuristic look.

With great excitement I boarded the Zephyr and, on arrival in Chicago, took a taxi to the Chicago Athletic Club where I was to stay during the competition. The cab ride was another first for me, but it didn't seem like a big deal at the time. Reflecting back, it was quite an accomplishment. At the age of 14, I made the journey to the big city alone. The other competitors had family members and coaches with them for support. In spite of all the challenges, I won the competition, and that victory qualified me to compete in the National Novice Division, also in Chicago. So later that year, I repeated my solo journey to Chicago and placed third, even after falling down during my performance.

In the summer of my fifteenth year, life was about to take an unexpected turn. It was a time when there was only one type of gasoline, and no cars came with automatic transmissions. All telephones were black; you spoke into mouthpiece and put a separate hearing device to your ear. Most homes had iceboxes with blocks of ice to keep food cold, and in many areas horse-drawn wagons still delivered bread, milk, and ice. There was no television and residential air-conditioning was years away, but in St. Paul, Minnesota, people could go to the Pop Concerts at the auditorium to be entertained and escape the oppressive summer heat.

The Pop Concerts were the inspiration of auditorium manager Ed Furni and the board of the St. Paul Figure Skating Club. Concerts were held three times a week and featured the seventy-piece Minneapolis Symphony, the St. Paul Civic Opera, and the St. Paul Figure Skating

Club. A different musical theme was featured each night. In addition to the Symphony, the best opera singers of the day sang, and skaters performed to wonderful arrangements of fine music. Folks could sit around rink-side tables under a beach umbrella and drink beer or pop, eat popcorn, and have a hot dog, all for a dollar. Or they could choose the balcony package and pay fifty cents.

Words still fail me when I attempt to describe the thrill of performing with a seventy-piece symphony to back me up. It was my third year performing in the Pop Concerts, and my coach, Viviane Hulten, had suggested the music I used that opening night. It was the Boston Pops version of the famous tango, "Jalousie." During the afternoon rehearsal, the orchestra leader asked what music I wanted to use for an encore. The thought of an encore had never crossed my mind. In fact, I had no idea what an encore was, so when he suggested I use Vincent Yeoman's "Tea for Two," I cheerfully agreed even though I'd never even heard the song before. In my naiveté it didn't occur to me that I should rehearse the number or at least hear the song. That evening when it was my time to perform, I skated to "Jalousie" as planned, and it went well. The audience called for an encore, and the strains of "Tea for Two" began. I started to skate, totally adlibbing. The music propelled me along, and I was totally alone on the ice in that sold-out, eight thousand-seat arena. It was just the music and me. . "Tea for Two" was a smooth and rhythmic dance number—no jumps or spins, just what turned out to be inspired footwork. I had no routine and no planned exit. When the time seemed right, I simply walked off the ice. As they say in show business, I stopped the show cold. The next day, I was front-page news in the entertainment section. During that summer I performed several times in later Pop Concerts with similar results

My amateur performance and Pops Concert appearances came to the attention of Lou Pieri, the treasurer of Ice Capades, who had seen me compete in the nationals and liked what he saw. He told John H. Harris, president of Ice Capades, about me. Shortly thereafter, John Harris contacted my father and told him the show was interested in hiring me. Dad was cool to the idea and said he wanted me to stay in school. Harris assured him that he understood, but invited my family to come and see the show, which was about to open in Chicago. They paid all expenses and gave us the red-carpet treatment. John Harris was there to persuade my father to enter into a contract. He proposed that I go on the road with the show when I was sixteen, just barely a year away and mentioned a figure that was more money than my father could imagine. I would have crawled over broken glass to leave that minute and join the show. I pleaded with my dad to agree, and finally we made a deal. I would go with the show at sixteen, stay for three years, then return to St. Paul, and go to college. I thought I'd finally out-witted my father because I *knew* there was no way I could get into any college with less than a year of high school.

It was 1942, and young men eighteen and older were joining the various military branches. The fact that I became male lead in Ice Capades was really the result of the war didn't register with me at the time. To be fair to myself, I was a good performer, but the show's male lead performer, Bobby Specht, was heading off to the air force. John Harris was buying insurance in the form of a sixteen-year-old apprentice that he could count on for at least a couple of years.

My trip from St. Paul to join Ice Capades in Hollywood was the start of many adventures to come. By now my father had remarried, and I had acquired a stepmother, Gertrude, who was to accompany me to Hollywood. I intensely disliked her and couldn't wait for her to finish her mission, go back to St. Paul, and allow me to be my own boss.

The Santa Fe Chief was the number three train in the Santa Fe line running from Chicago to Los Angeles, and like all the public trains at that time, its primary mission was carrying troops off to war. To this sixteen-year-old, however, when the conductor called out "aallll aboooard," it was a call to adventures beyond my wildest dreams. Not only was I headed for stardom in an ice show, but I could eat in the diner and didn't have to wash the dishes. I loved watching the lights of the little towns as we sped across the country and falling asleep to the clickity-clack of the wheels in my Pullman car bunk as my new life was unfolding. I had my first glimpse of palm trees and first heavenly smell of oranges when the train stopped in San Bernardino, California. Finally, we arrived at the grand, new Los Angeles Passenger Terminal (now called Union Station).

We checked into the Normandy Hotel not far from the Pan Pacific Auditorium where the show was rehearsing for the 1943 tour. I didn't know what to expect when I walked into that rink, but the spectacle of so many great skaters together in one place was a thrilling thing to behold. Even better, most of them were attractive young women. The average age of a Capades line skater was nineteen. I checked into the company office to let them know I was reporting for duty. They told me to go ahead and work out on the ice and get acquainted. My new partners had not yet arrived, but I did meet several other charming creatures who, I suspected, might have been checking me out too. I was a stranger in a strange land, and it was grand.

On My Own

After seeing me settled, Gertrude returned to St. Paul. Leo Loeb, a comedian in the show, offered to let me share his apartment with him. At the time, I didn't realize that John Harris had told him to take me under his wing and that I probably cramped his style at times, but we got along fine.

There was a lot to learn, and I had to learn it fast. I thought I had a clear idea of what was expected of me. I assumed I would skate and do a variety of jumps and spins. Instead, when I showed up for my first rehearsal, I was given a script and told to memorize it. I had to learn to pay attention to tight rehearsal schedules, show up on time, take direction from the choreographer and put on make up.

Program pictures for the new show were shot at the Republic Movie Studios by one of America's top photographers. There I learned that posing or performing for the pictures that ended up in the program required relentless repetition. Being an astute observer of things female, I learned that the girls' bosoms were made uniform in size by bust pads built into the costumes. We had a coffee stand backstage in each city where we could hang out between numbers for coffee or snacks. The company supplied the men with blue bathrobes; the girls with pink. Some of the girls decided to shock the young kid and used a gregarious chorus skater, Virginia, to be the vehicle. As I was sipping my coffee, she walked up to me and opened her robe. I remember the moment as if it were yesterday because that day I learned that some women have hair on their chests! I was stunned, and the girls couldn't stop laughing. I was putting in many long hours of hard work, but I was having the time of my life.

As an amateur, my only experience with costumes had been with those we rented from Geison's Rental Costumes in St. Paul for competitions and local amateur shows and consisted of tights, a white shirt, and tuxedo jacket. I thought they were grand indeed, but my introduction to professional ice show costuming took my breath away. Ice Capades had their own costume, office, and prop shop on Santa Monica Boulevard in Hollywood that was about the size of a modern grocery store. Once the production number was chosen, designers were invited to submit sketches, and the winner began to adapt the sketches to the figures of the various performers. During the war years, the first action was to obtain the materials to assure the costumes could be made. The nation's textile marts were scoured for the finest materials available. We were to have the best, not only because quality materials looked elegant and lasted longer, but they contributed to the appeal of the show as well as the moral of the performers.

Jewelers, wigmakers, milliners, tailors, fitters and a host of other skilled artisans produced the costumes. Dozens of seamstresses hunched over commercial sewing machines working on feathers, furs, silks, and sequins. The principal performers usually had three costumes for each number they performed. One was worn only for opening nights, another during the week, and a third for weekends. Two wardrobe women traveled with the show and devoted their time to costume maintenance and cleaning. I marveled at their skill and the quality of the materials. To me, these specialized theatrical costumers were magicians.

After completing the rehearsals and program pictures, just before we left Hollywood, I was introduced to the public for the first time as an Ice Capader. Each year at the end of their stay in Hollywood, the show's stars "volunteered" their time to perform a Gala "Silver Skates" Benefit for the *Los Angeles Herald Examiner*. I arranged for the orchestra to play my amateur numbers, the French tango "Jalousie" followed by "Tea for Two." Once again, I stopped the show and had a number of encores.

2. Donna Atwood, Phil Taylor, Jimmy Lawrence, Bobbie Specht, Nate Walley, Ice Capades, 1943

That night I learned important lessons about the real world and particularly the real world of Ice Capades. First, I learned that the show owner's interest might not be the same as mine, and in any conflict of interest, he was going to prevail every time. The show's owner, John H. Harris, had a special interest in Donna Atwood, whom he eventually married. He would not allow another soloist to receive more attention than her. Second, my "Tea for Two" number had what is known in the trade as a "walk off," which Orin Markhus and Irma Thomas, The Old Smoothies, always used to close their number. I was never allowed to do a smooth and sophisticated number again, only numbers that were fast and dynamic, which I didn't enjoy as much. Even so, the "Rythmic Bombshell" (as I was billed) went over very well, but intricate footwork was my specialty, and I never felt I reached my full potential. Not long after the atomic bombs were dropped in the summer of 1945, my billing was upgraded to the "Rythmatomic Bombshell."

Following our stint in Hollywood, we were scheduled to do two break-ins (trial performances) of the show, and then break for two weeks' vacation before our formal grand opening in New York's Madison Square Garden in September. The two break-in towns were Portland, Oregon, and Seattle.

The break-in engagements enabled us to tighten up the show and trim it to exactly two and one-half hours so it was an efficient, smooth-running machine. The master of ceremonies timed each number to be sure that none ran longer or shorter than their allotted times. In the East it was especially important for the show to always run on time so the commuters could catch their trains for home.

The train trip from Los Angeles to Portland will always be memorable. We traveled on the Southern Pacific "Daylight," and I saw Mt. Shasta and the Cascades for the first time. My father did the advertising for the Minnesota Tourist Bureau, and I grew up believing that Minnesota and its wondrous lakes was the end-all of the world's sceneries. I was taken by the beauty of both Portland and Seattle and realized that the country held many more wonders. Both engagements went well for me, and I was beginning to settle in as a real pro at the tender age of sixteen.

I returned to St. Paul, performed in a few of the summer ice shows for the Pop Concerts, and just enjoyed basking in my newfound stardom locally. Then it was on to New York about a week ahead of the show. I was to report to costumers for fitting of new costumes. My home for the three-week New York engagement was the Lincoln Hotel in Manhattan, near Times Square. As I was in charge of my own diet, I ate hot fudge sundaes in their coffee shop three times a day. Fortunately, I was still able maintain my 140–145 pound weight.

Our premiere run in New York's Madison Square Garden was three weeks and, of course, I will always remember that opening night. My dad came down from St. Paul for the big event. At sixteen, I had no idea how big an event it really was. The St. Paul Auditorium seated about eight thousand, while Madison Square Garden at that time was around eighteen thousand. When you were performing, however, the difference was not that apparent, and I lacked the experience and sophistication to know or even care that Walter Winchell and the major members of the New York press were evaluating my performance. I just remember that I stepped out on the ice alone in the glare of the spotlights, I stayed on my feet, I got through my numbers, and the reviews were good.

The Founders

The major shows were Ice Follies, Ice Capades, and Holiday on Ice. These companies toured year round, subsequently had at least one subsidiary show, and all but Ice Follies eventually played internationally. Holiday on Ice became the dominant show outside the United States with three or four shows in Europe, behind the Iron Curtain, Asia, Africa, South America, and Australia. All three major shows played in virtually every city in the United States, Canada, and Mexico. Initially, they played only in cities that had arenas with permanent indoor artificial ice, but with the advent of Holiday on Ice and its use of portable ice rinks (tanks), all the shows played in most cities with populations large enough to warrant a show's appearance. Both Ice Capades and Holiday on Ice played on outdoor baseball fields, soccer fields, and bullrings. Ice Follies tended to stay in the traditional arenas and auditoriums.

Sonja Henie had been making appearances between periods at hockey games and at the Center Theater in Radio City, New York. The Center Theater was a permanent, year-around ice show on the stage, more like the Broadway musicals as opposed to the grand touring shows. Not long after the launching of Ice Follies, Sonja took her show, the

Sonja Henie Hollywood Review on the road, however her show only toured a few months during the year.

Shipstads And Johnson—Ice Follies

Roy and Eddy Shipstads and Oscar Johnson lived in St. Paul, Minnesota and spent all of their spare time skating on Lake Como and other frozen lakes and ponds in St. Paul and the surrounding area. The Shipstads came from a family of nine. Hearing that Swedish was spoken in St. Paul their father emigrated from Sweden and settled in St. Paul. He was a molder in a foundry in St. Paul. Oscar Johnson had a similar background and lived a few blocks from the Shipstads. Mrs. Shipstad often complained that her boys were spending too much time on the ice and needed to go out and get some *real* jobs.

About the time of Sonja's American debut in 1936, the Shipstad brothers, Roy and Eddie, and Oscar Johnson took the first viable ice show on the road. Ice Follies first engagement was in Tulsa, Oklahoma, but paid attendance was thin opening night. Oscar Johnson encouraged the cast not to be nervous because they would outnumber the audience.

An aspect of the launching of Ice Follies that has received very little recognition is the role of a skilled public relations man, Russ Mulckey. Russ became friendly with the Shipstads and Oscar Johnson while they were performing at the Sherman Hotel's College Inn in Chicago. Many credit him as being instrumental in aiding the Shipstads with the business and PR acumen that they lacked. In the formation and planning of Ice Follies, he was an essential driving force as the show survived and gained recognition. Unfortunately, Russ had an untimely death, and his widow received little for his contribution to the show.

Sonja Henie—The Sonja Henie Review

Wilhelm Henie (Sonja Henie's father) was the driving force behind Sonja's early success both as an amateur and as a professional. Henie had amassed a large fortune as a furrier in Norway, and the family's lifestyle paralleled that of royalty. Unlike the rags to riches stories circulated about the Norwegian wunderkind, Sonja lacked for nothing and was the family's center of attention. Father Henie carefully cultivated relationships with many of the figure skating judges which assured her numerous first place finishes, particularly in the 1936 Olympics. That year Viviane Hulten of Sweden was a strong contender who many thought should have won.

Henie viewed his daughter's skating as a business from the beginning—the end justifying the means. An astute businessman and personal manager, he managed his daughter's exposure in Europe's largest ice rinks as one might develop a great star of the opera or symphonic world. He brought Sonja to the United States, rented rinks in which she would perform, worked the press like a pro, and booked her for performances between periods at hockey games. The public loved the cute, perky Scandinavian, and make no mistake, Sonja was a fine skater with some superb innovations of her own. Probably the most far reaching of these was that, from the time of her childhood, she envisioned performing highlights of the great operas on ice. No question, Sonja was a great performer, and the ice arena managers began to notice attendance at their hockey games rising dramatically, and some were coming to see the little Norwegian's figure skating exhibitions perhaps as much or more than the hockey.

Wilhelm and Sonja noticed this development, and Wilhelm rented the Polar Palace ice arena in Hollywood and produced Sonja's Hollywood Ice Revue to introduce his daughter to the movie industry, thus setting the stage for Sonja's career to take shape in several directions at the same time. Arthur Wirtz, a successful grain trader in Chicago who also controlled the Chicago Stadium became her partner and backed her show. He obtained the US franchise for Vat 69 Scotch whiskey for Sonja and advised her to buy land just south of Los Angeles known as Signal Hill. Shortly after the purchase of Signal Hill, oil was discovered there helping to make Sonja the wealthiest woman in Hollywood.

John H. Harris and The Arena Managers Association—Ice Capades

A critical force in this evolution of touring ice shows was the need of American ice arena managers to fill seats in their arenas when their hockey teams weren't playing. On Valentine's Day in 1940, the nine-member Arena Managers Association met in Hershey, PA, with the intention forming a new ice show, later called Ice Capades. John H. Harris, of the Pittsburgh Gardens, was president. The other members were Walter A. Brown of the Boston Gardens; Louis A. R. Pieri of the Rhode Island Auditorium; Louis Jacobs, the Buffalo Auditorium; John Sollenberger, the Hershey Sports Arena; Al Sutphin, the Cleveland Arena; Edward W. Shore, the Springfield Coliseum; Peter A. Tyrell, the Philadelphia Arena; Nathan Podoloff, the New Haven Arena. Walter Brown was vice president and treasurer and Lou Pieri, secretary. The others were directors.

Pete Tyrell was designated business manager and tasked to organize and sign talent for the first show. Each of the stockholders put up five thousand dollars to launch this venture. The investment would later be worth millions.

Each of these men owned or controlled hockey teams, but were motivated to explore opportunities for enhancing arena revenues with other events. They had seen Sonja Henie's popular appeal when appearing between periods at their hockey games and witnessed the success Shipstad and Johnson were beginning to have with Ice Follies in their arenas and elsewhere. The arena managers had access to the books and could see a major opportunity. Rehearsals were to start that May at John Harris's Pittsburgh Gardens Arena.

Unlike Follies or Sonja's Shows, Ice Capades' owners were not skaters. They viewed the show as an investment. Nevertheless, John Harris was driven to have the best show on the road. The first edition of Ice Capades in 1940–41 had an all-star cast, as did Ice Follies. The featured performer was the great English star Belita (Belita Jeppson Turner). Belita was a gorgeous woman and was years ahead of her time. She combined an extensive dance background with exceptional figure skating skills. Her costuming was of her own design and far superior to what the other female skaters were offering. She had a sense of business that enabled her to drive contract bargains to her advantage. Megan Taylor, the English and a former World Champion, and Robin Lee, a five-time US champion were in the show along with a stable of other fine performers. These included: Robert Dench and Rosemarie Stewart, English pair skating champions; Al Surette; Denise and Pierre Benoit;

Lois Dworshak; McGowan and Mack; Cliff and Rona Thael; and Phil Taylor. Donna Atwood, US singles and pair champion, joined the show in 1942 and became the featured star. Donna later married John Harris and bore him twin sons, Dinnie and Donny, and a daughter, Sissy.

Holiday on Ice

In December of 1943, Chicago-based theatrical agent Carl Snyder and dance director Don Arden launched a brand new ice show scheduled to play during the holidays in Toledo, Ohio. Because the show was primarily a holiday attraction, they named it *Holiday on Ice*. It was so well received they repeated it the next year. As Holiday's identity was evolving, two Milwaukee brothers were in the wings with a dream of taking an ice show on the road with its own large portable ice rink. Emery and Cal Gilbert, owners of the Ace Box Lunch Company, had heard about Holiday on Ice. The neophyte owners knew that the established shows, Capades and Follies, controlled arenas, and Sonja Henie had the large arenas provided by her partner Arthur Wirtz. The Gilberts understood their only option was to play buildings in the South and southeast, which had no ice. They sold their business and put all of their resources in a third Holiday touring show staged on a large portable rink (called a tank in the ice show parlance). The show was very successful, but touring was inefficient because it took more than a week to take the tank down and put it up in the next town. The solution was to buy another complete tank and leap frog the two units, so the show could tour like Follies and Capades.

There was just one problem; the Gilberts didn't have the money for a second tank.. An ice rink tank isn't an actual tank, but several miles of piping carrying a refrigerant sufficient to cover an area approximately 100 x 60 feet or larger with its own compressors. Semi trailers and drivers were required to move the tanks, and technicians and refrigeration engineers were needed to make it all happen. As you can imagine, we are talking major money.

In 1945, Morris Chalfen of Minneapolis became aware of the Gilbert brothers' tank dilemma. Chalfen was the consummate entrepreneur and promoter and shared the Gilbert's passion for ice shows. However, there was no market left for him in which to launch an ice show in the United States. So Chalfen and his partner, Harold Steinman, produced the first roller skating show, Skating Vanities, in 1942.

Chalfen met with the Gilbert brothers, solved their money problem, and took over the show. Chalfen used the best production talent that money could buy from all over the country, borrowing from both Ice Capades and the Sonja Henie show for production talent. The show was a success and made several movies. It was a good partnership. Chalfen had the money, business acumen, and show business experience, and the Gilberts had the technical expertise. This was the beginning of what would eventually become the largest ice show conglomerate in the world, with shows in every corner of the world.

The Companies—No Two Alike

Each company had its own personality. The final product was a result of the personal vision of the founders of each company.

Ice Follies

The policy of Shipstads and Johnson was to present their product as a family-oriented all-star show, and they had some great performers. Most ice show fans were well acquainted with Roy and Eddie Shipstad and Oscar Johnson and later with Roy's wife, Bess Erhardt. The emphasis on family applied off the ice as well as on, to a degree not found in any of the other shows. Eddie Shipstad's wife was deeply religious, so there was a focus on morality among the cast members. They had such things as company-sponsored bowling leagues, which none of the other shows had. The owners' participation in the social activities of the cast also tended to create an environment different from the other shows.

Follies focused on superb professional performers whether they held amateur medals or not. Besides Shipstads and Johnson and Bess Erhardt, other skaters included Evelyn Chandler, Bruce Mapes, Fran Claudet, Osborn Colson, Harris and Phyliss Legg, Ruby and Bobby Maxson, and Frick and Frack. The Follies also emphasized quality skating, resulting in one of the most capable chorus lines of any of the shows. They regularly featured members of the ensemble as trios, quartets, and quintets.

The Ice Follies had beautiful costumes, quality musical arrangements, fine sets, innovative choreography, and one feature that none of the other shows achieved—remote-controlled props. Eddie Shipstad was a relentless gadgeteer and was the first to develop and use radio-controlled props on the ice. At Eddie's home in Encino, CA, the bathroom contained a remote controlled toilet that when occupied could be moved from its normal location to the hall, causing embarrassment for those using the facility.

At the end of an engagement in Portland one year, four Ice Follies performers rented a car to drive to San Francisco and were involved in a tragic accident killing all four skaters. From that time on, the company prohibited performers from driving during the tour. Horseback riding and skiing were also forbidden.

Sonja Henie Review

The Sonja Henie Ice Review was unique in that its founder was also its featured performer, and by design no other performer was allowed, even for a moment, to outshine the star. This was not by contract, but all members of the Henie show knew the rules. All the shows had performance directors who watched each show for quality maintenance. However, in the case of the Henie Review, the performance director had the additional task of being alert to whether anyone in the show was beginning to surface as an audience attraction in which case they would either eliminate their number or fire the performer. That is not to say that Sonja did not have other acts but no other star skaters per se. Freddy Trenkler, one of the great ice comedians, appeared with her, as did Fritz Dietl, a stilt skater, and other novelty acts. One of the great mainstays of the Henie show was an English slapstick comedy act called the Bruises that both

Ice Capades and Ice Follies later mimicked. It was often copied, but never quite equaled. The trio members were Sid Spaulding, Geoff Stevens, and Monte Scott. Sid went on to become a highly regarded cinematographer and received a number of awards for innovations he developed in cinematography.

One of the trademarks of Sonja's show was her partners, and over the years she had a stable of tall handsome partners. Most were excellent experienced show skaters; however, in her show their role was to present her in the prima-donna star tradition. Rumor has it that some may have performed duties off the ice to keep her spirits up, along with another rumor that she kept a case of champagne in her dressing room to quench her thirst between numbers.

Her first partner was Jackie Dunn, an Englishman, who skated with Sonja for two years after she came to America. In 1939, Dunn died of rabbit fever. It was not a well-kept secret that he was also her lover of the moment. A series of partners followed, including Harrison Thompson (England), Gene Theslof (Finland), Michael Kirby, a respected Canadian champion, and Marshall Beard. Marshall grew up in the famous Hershey school for orphans. He had extensive experience, having performed with virtually all the ice shows during his career. Marshall also saved Sonja from a career collapse.

When Sonja married Dan Topping, he persuaded her to break her relationship with Arthur Wirtz, who had guided her career to heights that were soon lost with Topping at the helm.

After the break with Wirtz, Topping in the driver's seat created a disaster that saw her show unevenly booked and the loss of Wirtz controlled arenas forced Sonja to do tank dates in outdoor locations. One night at one of her last tank performances, in a stadium in Baltimore, the bleachers collapsed, causing numerous injuries. Subsequent lawsuits haunted Sonja, and the need to pay them off forced her to attempt to play in still worse settings.

Sonja's ex-partner, Marshall Beard, became aware of her tragic situation and contacted Morris Chalfin. Chalfin had admired Sonja and hoped that, in some way, he might someday be able to work with her. After Beard's call, Chalfin contacted Sonja, and under the auspices of Holiday on Ice in Europe, they put together a successful tour. Beard was her last partner and was instrumental in allowing her to finish her career as a great star.

Ice Capades

Ice Capades followed the Ice Follies format, but while Follies emphasized quality skating, Ice Capades focused on the entertainment package. They also adopted the prohibitions against driving, skiing, and horseback riding on tour and were interested in what cast members were doing off the ice. They gathered personal information by having cast member informants in both the men's and women's dressing rooms. The informants gathered information that might be useful as leverage during contract time or as a means of preventing cast members from gaining any advantage over management. The company manager, reportedly, sent a coded telegram daily to John Harris giving him information about gate receipts as well as any personal information that might be of interest to him.

Holiday on Ice

In the fifties, the number one unit of Holiday on Ice was about the same size as both Ice Capades and Ice Follies; however, the environment in this show was quite different from either Capades or Follies. While Capades and Follies had a number of rules that its cast members had to follow to the letter, Holiday only required that you be on time for your performance, and although they provided transportation, many of the cast drove personal automobiles or pulled trailers. In other words, it was less like an ice show and more like one of the touring stage shows. Their product was top quality, and the performers were treated more like adults and less like commodities whose main value was to make money for the owners. In fairness to Capades and Follies, the average age of ensemble members was eighteen or nineteen, so there could be arguments made for their personnel strategies. Like the other shows, Holiday originally had some fine performers, such as Dorothy Goos,

Murray Galbraith, Kay Servatius, Jacqueline DuBief, Paul Andre, Jinx Clark, Tommy Collins, Don Watson, Arnold Shoda, and Guy Longpre.

Holliday on Ice and much of the ice skating community was devastated in 1960 when a Northwest Airlines plane carrying Marty Chalfen, wife of owner Morris Chalfen, and sister of Tommy Collins, disintegrated in flight over Tell City, Indiana. Marty had been a skater in the show and was traveling with their children, Linda, Martha, and Richard. All were lost, but the cause of the explosion was never discovered.

Three years later, Holliday experienced another terrible tragedy when an explosion, apparently caused by a gas leak, killed sixty-three people just minutes after the end of the show on opening night in Indianapolis, Indiana.

The Business

Booking the Shows

In retrospect, the launching of both Ice Follies and Ice Capades may appear to have been an easy undertaking. It wasn't! Both shows tilted with disaster at least once before they found their groove. Our major American ice shows were large complex organisms with operating costs that would terrify the faint of heart. If the founders fully understood what they were getting into, in the beginning they might well have tried something else.

The Ice Capades and Ice Follies had advantages that Holiday on Ice lacked, they had bookings, scheduling, and a non-compete agreement for talent. These were used to great advantage. Control of most of the major arenas enabled them to manage their scheduling efficiently, which, in turn, kept transportation costs under control. The issue of scheduling locations close together was important because there was no income for the owners when over a hundred skaters were merely enjoying the scenery or playing cards on a train. The booking tool also allowed the Arena Managers Association, in concert with Ice Follies, to keep newcomers out of the business and enabled the two shows to avoid playing a given city too close together, thus maximizing profits.

The Union

There was a "Closed Shop" in the ice show unions of the forties and fifties. You had to belong to the American Guild of Variety Artists (AGVA), or you didn't skate. Dues were deducted from the paychecks every week.

During our run in Atlantic City, we usually shot advertising commercials for Philco with their new radios and gadgets. It was a part of our contract. We didn't get paid and didn't even get a free radio. Today it would have been worth major money.

It wasn't until many years later that we began to suspect that the AGVA was a creation of the show owners and its primary function was to forewarn management of unrest among the skaters. When Bobby Kennedy became Attorney General, he began to enforce antitrust legislation and the union farce was one of a number of sins that came to light. Yes, things changed dramatically after Kennedy prevailed in the suit.

Payday

The average age of the performers in the great American ice shows was nineteen. Most of those nineteen-year-olds came from families with no sophistication in professional contract negotiations and had no idea as to the value those young skaters provided to the show owners. Thus contract negotiations were between shrewd businessmen and neophytes. The salaries offered seemed unbelievable to the skaters and their families and, as noted later, were about a fifth or less of what the performers might have realized if they'd had access to professional managers or an understanding of the values involved. Professional managers did not appear on the scene until the shows began to hire

Olympic or World Champions in the seventies. Generally, the performers were having the time of their lives and thought they had received a piece of the moon. Ice Capades performers were paid weekly but had to submit a detailed personal expense form from the previous week before receiving their paychecks. At the end of the year, the show had their own accountants prepare the performers' tax returns. Line skaters (chorus members) usually spent every penny they made and had to write home for money for train or airfare to get home for the three-week summer break and back again.

When Robert Kennedy began to pursue and win antitrust suits against a number of corporations, the unspoken noncompete agreement between the ice shows went away. In 1957 prior to the suit principal skaters made an average of $300 per week during the time we were on tour. There was no extra pay for holidays and no vacation pay. During the three weeks of rehearsel, we received half our salary. I retired from the show that year and my successor was able to negotiate his salary and made over $4,000 per week. Income from the endorsements and public appearances which had previously benefited the company now went to him This resulted in a substantial increase in income for many principal performers. The effect of the litigation had no impact on ticket prices, and the promoters still did well.

The Ice Show Family

Partners

Standing in an elegant ballroom in Las Vegas in June 2000, surrounded by seven hundred current and former Ice Capades performers at our fiftieth reunion, I especially looked forward to seeing one person, Donna Atwood Harris. I first met Donna fifty-seven years before when I was sixteen. I was uncertain whether we would recognize each other. I finally found her sitting at a table, surrounded by some other graying former performers. She greeted me warmly. The face had changed little. However, she now walked haltingly with a cane due to a painful hip ailment.

We didn't discuss those years of skating together. Instead, we talked about our current activities and our families. Sadly that was the last time I saw Donna. She died in December 2010.

Donna was eighteen and the female lead in Ice Capades when I first met her. The previous year she had won the US pair-skating championship with Gene Turner as well as the Pacific Coast ladies' singles championship. Like me, she was largely self-taught and because all competitions had been canceled after the start of WWII, opportunities for amateur conquests were no longer available. I had been hired to be her partner and the male lead in the show. I was five foot seven, and she was five foot four. I weighed 143 pounds, and she weighed 112. I would be required to do overhead lifts with her. I knew nothing about pair skating and had no idea how I was going to manage. But Donna, in a gentle way, taught me the rudiments of pair skating, and we soon developed a good working relationship. We worked well together for the next two years.

She was the first of four partners in my years in the ice show business. The second, Virginia Baxter, had been an Olympic medalist, who died too young with cancer. The third, Anne Robinson, had been a national junior champion.

Margaret Field became my wife and the mother of my two wonderful children and was my fourth and last partner.

3. Donna Atwood and Jamie Lawrence, 1943

The show format that first year remained the same for all my partners and me throughout my career. My partner and I were responsible for the pair number in the feature production at the end of the first half of the show. Then, we performed another pair in the costume number in the middle of the second half. We would do the choreography together for the pair number, and each choreographed our own solos. Between us, we accounted for one hour of the two and a half hour show.

That year's feature production was *Song of the Islands*, which was arguably the first story on ice. For its South Sea Island theme, much research was done to assure the costumes, sets, dancing, and music were authentic. The company hired a Hawaiian singer, Al Kikuume, to sing, and Donna did a wicked hula. I was Prince Taluga, dressed in a loincloth, wearing a long wig and pursuing Princess Tahita, played by Donna. The worst injury of my career occurred during that pair number when Donna hooked the heel of her blade in my shin and laid it open from ankle to knee. Prince Taluga finished the number, trailing blood all over the rink. Backstage, after the number, the company nurse applied butterfly bandages, and I went on to do my numbers in the second half.

In our second year together, the feature production was Si Si, *Fiesta* a great production number in which strobe lights were used to create a dazzling impression of the skaters becoming part of a great Spanish shawl. I played the role of a toreador, she the bull with a horned head-dress. The show hired Edwardo Cansino to train me in the use of the cape and picadors. Edwardo was part of the famous Spanish Cansino dance family. Movie audiences knew his niece, Margarita, as Rita Hayworth. The costumes were fabulous and in a press release, the company listed materials used in their construction. These included: 34 million spangles, 8,000 yards of cotton lace and organdies, 4,000 yards of rayon and satins, 7,000 yards of Conti-Glo (flourescent) material, 400 yards of velvets, 4,200 yards of cotton materials, 1,500 yards of felt, 2,500 yards of wool fringe, 400 yards of crepe, 1,200 yards of hand embroidered lace, 1,500 leather skins, 1,000 pieces of hand made jewelry

We received excellent reviews and made the covers of several prominent national magazines.

4. Virginia "Gini" Baxter, Jimmy Lawrence

Virginia Baxter was a United States and Olympic medalist from Detroit. In 1952 she easily won the free skating portion in the Olympics. She was five foot two, with short blond hair and was truly a free spirit. Sometimes I could not resist ad-libbing my own lyrics to the songs we were supposed to be singing. They could be rather irreverent at times, and that delighted her. I heard that, like some men, she kept a black book recording her male conquests (no, it did not include me). Of all my partners, she was the strongest and most capable skater and had the best feel for getting into character. We performed *Brigadoon* that year, and of all the numbers I've done, it is easily the most memorable because of its haunting melodies. I played the role of Tommy, and Gini was Fiona. We performed a pair to "Come to Me, Bend to Me," and I did a solo to "Heather on the Hill." Our orchestra leader, Jerry Mayhall, composed a particularly compelling arrangement of the music. Even after four hundred performances, I never tired of the music. It seemed to lift our performance to new heights. I have heard that Gini's life after the ice show was an unhappy one, sadly culminating with breast cancer. She was a vibrant gal, and I miss her.

When I returned to the show in 1949 after three years in college, I was partnered with Margaret Field to perform in Empress Hall in Earls Court, London. We performed *Snow White and the Seven Dwarfs*. It was not one of my favorite numbers. There was a door in the middle of the façade of the Snow White set, and Margaret and came through the door, lip-synching to "With a Smile and a Song." We would pause for a moment while trained pigeons flew up from the ice and land on our wrists.

After a few seconds, we gently waved them off and walked down two steps to the ice to do a pair number while stagehands retrieved the pigeons. Except for one time. Somehow, one night, the pigeon removal was overlooked, and they were still on the ice when, after our pair, I swung around in front of the set to start my solo and ran right through the middle of the flock. I can't say who was more startled, the pigeons or the "Prince." I can tell you that none of us was injured.

5. Margaret Field and Jimmy Lawrence, American in Paris

Next year, our production number was *An American in Paris*, one of the best numbers I ever performed. *Billboard Magazine* wrote that it was "one of the strongest bits of ice ballet choreography ever in the show." The company hired Fred Kelly, whose brother Gene starred in the movie version, to work with me on the choreography and help me learn some of his brother's moves from the movie. Fred looked like Gene's twin. Fred was as good dancer as Gene, but didn't make it in the movies because he wasn't as photogenic.

Espania Mombo, was the featured number the next year and, along with *The Student Prince*, would also be among my all time favorite numbers.

About Pair Skating

There are four types of pair skating: shadow pairs, adagio, ice dancing, and standard pairs, which may be a combination of the other three types. My partners and I did standard pair skating. In addition to skill and timing, there must be trust in order to be successful as team.

A shadow pair is what the name implies. Two people, who may or may not be of the same gender, do a routine together on the ice without touching one another. This is not an element in the competitions, but was often done in ice shows.

Adagio pair skating is an entirely different level of physics. It involves a male built like an Olympic weightlifter and a petite female. Their routines involve a lot of acrobatic lifts, carries, and throws that demand impeccable timing, I remember, one adagio pair - a married couple. She was rather serene, but he was quite impulsive and could be volatile. While we were playing a city in the Midwest, they had a disagreement in their hotel room, and he apparently thought that by holding her outside the window by one leg he would win the argument. Fortunately, he had a strong grip and their room was on the first floor, so no one was injured.

Until 1984, ice dancing was generally considered rather dull—an activity for older skaters. In competition, the first segment contained prescribed dances, the last was free dance. Here skaters could be innovative but with two restrictions: they must remain within an arm's length at all times and were not allowed to do overhead lifts. Torvil and Dean elevated ice dancing to new heights at the 1984 Olympics. They did the prescribed dances with flair that would have enabled them to win any competition easily, but when they did the free dance, hearts of skaters the world over stopped cold for four minutes while they watched transfixed to maybe the most moving skating performances of all time. No pair had ever skated like that before. Their performance was technically flawless, and the artistry, choreography, and use of music were stunning.

Chorus Line

So many male performers had answered the call to war that the male chorus line—the Ice Cadets—was virtually wiped out. Ice Capades replaced them with girls for those years. They added forty-two girls, selected from over four thousand girls who auditioned for the positions from all parts of the country, and created the biggest chorus line in the business. The chorus line consisted of three classes of skaters based on their height. In ice show parlance of that day, line girls five foot two or shorter were referred to as "ponies." Girls five foot two to five foot eight were called the forty-eight line because they used forty-eight girls in that height group. Girls five foot eight and over were showgirls. In total there were ninety girls in the chorus, and their average age was nineteen. In today's politically correct atmosphere, line "girls" would probably be called women of the ensemble.

In 1944, the show producers wanted the chorus line to open the show with big production number paying tribute to the Marine Corps. They were looking for something authentic and spectacular, and they wanted perfection. The Marine Corps helped by assigning a veteran Marine Master Drill Sergeant, Frank French, to train the girls. The Marine was a survivor of the battle of Guadalcanal and had been recuperating from malaria at a military hospital in California. He said when the orders came through to report to Ice Capades, he dismissed it as a joke. For six weeks, he drilled the ladies relentlessly in front of the arena and taught them the manual of arms. This hard-nosed guy was used to talking to marines, but he tried his best to curtail his salty language around young women and only bellowed at them once for getting the giggles over some distraction.

The number was a huge success when the show opened in Madison Square Garden, as it was with audiences across the country. The next year, they hired a senior Canadian Mountie instructor to train the girls in the Canadian equivalent of a rifle drill, again, with impressive results.

Military themes were dropped after the war, and as materials were no longer rationed, the costumes became even more elaborate. An example of the new emphasis on opulence was a finale we did after the war, which I would always remember. All the line skaters were dressed in white evening dress with full-length *genuine sable stoles*. The males had white tails, top hats, and canes. My partner, Margaret Field, and I were dressed in a similar fashion, and with the entire company on the ice, I drove us around the rink in a pink XK120 Jaguar. At the end of the number, we got out and took the final bow with the rest of the cast.

Comedians

Esco Larue was a Cree Indian from Oklahoma. Oil had been discovered on his family's land, and the family became wealthy. Esco was six foot two and muscular. He loved to gamble and hung out with gamblers in every city. He was tough, but had a heart of gold and was a dear friend. Esco's life was show business, and he developed a comedy number that was hilarious and very popular. He didn't wear skates but sat in the audience acting like a drunk, and then staggered onto the ice during an adagio pair number creating mayhem with the skaters.

Esco was a good guy with a terrific sense of humor. One evening, we were having dinner in the Lord Nelson Hotel in Halifax, Nova Scotia. As the cast gathered for dinner after the show, Esco was wearing a pair of fake eyeballs on springs. He convinced the waitresses in their black uniforms with starched white aprons that with those eyeballs he could see through people's clothes. The dining room had large pillars, and before long all the waitresses were hiding behind the pillars. Esco fell over backward in his chair attempting to peer behind the pillars.

Joe Jackson, Jr. was one of the all-time great pantomime comedians and a member of the cast of the first Ice Capades. Like Esco Larue, he performed his act without skates. Joe's father, a former Austrian cycling champion, had developed and performed the act all around the world. and Joe Jr. carried on the tradition. In his act, Joe dressed like a tramp with big floppy shoes. He came on the ice with a bicycle that began to fall apart. As he attempted to reassemble the bicycle, he got the parts in the wrong places. He placed the sprocket where the seat should be and then proceeded to mount the bike. Next to my numbers, it was my father's favorite act in the show. I sometimes wonder if maybe my dad even liked Joe's act better. Joe performed the act all over the world and made many television appearances.

Eric Waite was a figure-skating comic. He and his brother Norton learned to skate on the rinks and ponds in Alberta. In Eric's most popular number, he dressed as a little girl and always had the audience rolling in the aisles with his comic antics. Tragically, Eric had a terrible auto accident in which he was thrown from the car and sustained a crushed pelvis. The doctor told him he would never skate again. In his determination, he proved them wrong. They wired his pelvis together and he returned to the show. When he skated, however, the wires heated up causing intense pain. In spite of the pain, he continued to perform and was always a real crowd pleaser. The only sour note might be that he did drink a lot and had a tendency to become rather mean at times. I often wonder why some comics I have known were jolly and friendly on the ice, but mean and unpleasant off the ice.

Larry Jackson and Bernie Lynam were two of the meanest people I have ever met. They had a slapstick comedy number and were known as Jackson and Lynam. Jackson was one of those people who would bully those who didn't have power, in his case, usually chorus skaters. Bernie Lynam was just slimy mean. Jackson and Lynam had pirated their slapstick act from a comedy trio in the Sonja Henie Ice Show called the Bruises. I warmly recall an incident when we were changing trains in Chicago. Three of the line skaters were getting into a cab. Jackson shoved them out of the way to take the cab for himself. The Chicago cab driver got out of the cab and knocked Jackson flat on his back. The girls got into cab and left Jackson lying in the street. My heart sang, and people nearby applauded.

Howard "Sully" Sullivan was from Escanaba in Michigan's upper peninsula. Like me, he joined the show when he was sixteen. He started in the chorus but soon developed a comedy act of his own and later teamed up with Leo Loeb. He married my wife's sister Beverley, got a degree in engineering, and became an engineer with the California State Highway Department. He was an extrovert who talked nonstop and was always entertaining. Anytime he had an incident to relate, he couldn't help but act out the story with great energy and played the part of each character involved. He was also a highly skilled artist. After his retirement and until his death, he would often show up for a visit, sometimes with other former skaters and we would reminisce into the early morning hours about the old days on the road.

Novelty Acts

Orin Markhus and Erma Thomas, *the* Old Smoothies were one of the show's strongest and most popular acts and performed just before the finale for many years. When not performing, Orin taught figure skating in St. Paul and supplemented his income by teaching golf at the Highland Park Golf Course. One of his pupils was Erma Thomas. He not only taught her how to golf, but also how to figure skate. That led to a successful partnership on the ice. Erma had three daughters, all of whom skated with Ice Follies. Two of the three were the famous Thomas Twins.

    Trixie Frischke is, to this day, a legend in juggling. She practiced every day without fail and under conditions that could be unpredictable; she was nearly flawless in performance. She had an amazing ability to incorporate acrobatics with juggling on skates. She was a shy person offstage, but in her performance, she projected great charisma, charm, and showmanship. Her father and sister, Hilda, sometimes traveled with her. Her father was a large man who managed her life and her finances and treated her like a vassal. He oversaw her daily practices and beat her when he thought her performance was not up to par. When she married Esco Larue, the beatings stopped. Esco suggested the father and sister might want to return to Hungary, and they were soon on their way. Although he was a great guy with a jolly sense of humor, it was never a good idea to provoke him.

    Marian "Red" McCarthy was an excellent interpretive skater and very creative. He performed on speed skates and put a lot of energy into his performances. "Red's" costume always consisted of a jock strap and an exotic headdress. He painted his entire body with a formula that was rumored to contain powdered glass and silver nitrate. It took him an hour to apply and at least as long to remove. The effects were spectacular and gave him an almost ghostly glow. He always kept the paint and equipment locked in a footlocker in the dressing room. One night, performing in a major eastern city, someone was able to get into the footlocker and put itching powder in his paint. As he skated and his pores started to open up, the powder began to have its effect. He never skated faster or jumped higher. Had he ever discovered the villain, without question, the peretrator would have been very sorry.

Another time, McCarthy developed a new number using black paint over his entire body with an exotic headdress. During a "break in" opening night benefit performance in Portland, Oregon, he sprinted down to the far end of the ice, stumbled, and fell into the front row occupied by Portland socialites. Many ladies had mink or sable fur coats on. When Red backed away from the front row, a lady with a white sable coat had two large black handprints on her chest. That was not part of the act!

6. Marion "Red" McCarthy

Al Surette dressed like a clown and his act was hilarious. His ability to contort his body in all sorts of different positions was unique and always delighted the audience. Like Eric Waite, Al was in constant pain due to a severe arthritic condition. He was a big-hearted guy who truly suffered for his art. His wife, Francis, was a nurse and visited the show periodically to give him gold shots to relieve his pain.

7. Al Surette

Hugh Forgie, from Brantford, Ontario, was an eleven-time world badminton champion. He turned pro and toured the country for several years in exhibition matches, taking on all challengers, then developed a skating clown act, and joined Ice Capades. His act included playing a one-man game, hitting the shuttlecock and then frantically sprinting to the alternate side of the net and hitting it back to himself. He claimed to have the game of badminton "down cold." He later worked as a team with Stig Larson.

8. Phil Taylor

Phil Taylor was born in the early nineteen hundreds on the wrong side of the tracks in London. He hung around ice rinks and learned to skate. He started his skating career as a barrel jumper and then decided it would be even more thrilling to skate on stilts. He became the originator of stilt skating on ice. From foot to ice, his stilts were about two feet high, made entirely of oak. He went on to develop an act for a stilt skating number where he was dressed as Johnny Walker like the figure on the whiskey bottle, monocle and all. When I worked with him, he was in his late forties. I always enjoyed his street wisdom. He and his daughter Megan were among the first Ice Capades performers. Megan had been a two-time world champion and was strong power skater. Over the years, I worked with several other stilt skaters, all much younger and all used high-tech metal stilts. But Phil Taylor was the original and in a class by himself.

Ted Meza had been a tap and eccentric dancer on the stage. He did a strange tap routine on the ice, which was mediocre. The one thing I remember about him was his dancing on a tabletop in the lobby of the Worth Hotel in Fort Worth the day Franklin Roosevelt died. I have never forgiven him.

The Burling Sisters were identical triplets, and although they were not all the same height, they really looked identical. They were sort of stair-stepped—short, medium, and tall—although tall just nudged five foot two. Each had electric red hair with a few freckles. Their pace of speaking was similar to that of a machine gun. They were never far apart and seemed to move like a school of fish or a flight of birds, anticipating each other's moves. They always dressed exactly alike and had a habit of completing each other's sentences. As a rule, when ice show producers had identical twins or triplets in their ranks, they would attempt to create a number for them in the show. The Burling triplets' skating skills did not warrant developing a featured number, but they were an attraction just because they were triplets. At the Ice Capades sixtieth reunion in Las Vegas, the Burlings were among the attendees. This time their spouses were in tow. Surprisingly, the sisters showed their age less than many of the rest of us. Just a few gray hairs sprinkled among the red. They still dressed exactly alike.

Cal Cook was a stilt skater. Before every performance, he would rush into the dressing room, slip his shoes off, and put on his stilts. After performing he would slip on the shoes and walk away. One evening he came in wearing a new pair of shoes with thick foam rubber soles. While he was on the ice, someone nailed his shoes to the floor. Cal rushed in after the performance, slipped his shoes on and started to walk away but instead fell flat on his face. To this day, Cal would still like to find the perpetrator.

Roommates

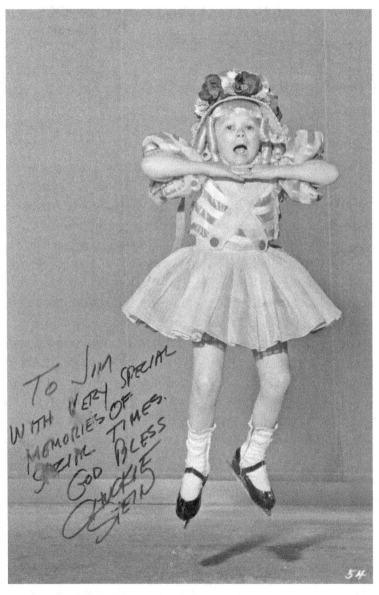

9. Chuckie Stein

Chuckie Stein, my first regular roommate, was from Pittsburgh, a devout Catholic, and four feet tall. He was twenty-two years old, but physically, the size of a ten-year-old boy. It was also his first year in the show. He had been an usher in one of John Harris's theaters. Harris also owned the Pittsburgh Hornets Hockey team and asked Chuckie to be their mascot. He took to skating like a natural, and before long, Harris asked him to join the show. Over the years, he played the role of many of Disney's animals on the ice. After retiring from the show, he went to the Mayo Clinic in Rochester, Minnesota, to undergo a risky procedure that enabled him to grow a foot taller. He married a few years later and became a councilman in Pittsburgh. He was a kind and gentle person and loyal friend, and we stayed in touch until his death in 2003.

The Hollywood stay each year was something the cast looked forward to with great anticipation. We had a homelike environment and could cook food at home. As a special treat when we were rehearsing, we could go out in the evenings to see movies at the numerous drive-ins in the Hollywood area. When we came back to Hollywood at the end of the tour that first year, Chuckie and I and several other cast members rented Jack Oakie's home in the San Fernando Valley. It was not uncommon for movie stars who needed money to rent out their homes. I decided I would lease a car to use during our stay. I was seventeen and had no driving experience or instruction. I wrote to a friend in Minnesota who bought a license for me for twenty-five cents. He mailed me the license, and I rented a 1941 blue Buick super convertible and drove it off the lot. How or why I didn't kill myself or somebody else I will never know.

The next year our group rented a different home, also belonging to a star. The home was a gorgeous Spanish-style mansion in Hollywood with a pool surrounded by plants that gave the look and sensation of being in the heart of a jungle.

Henry Barnicle, the drummer with our show, was my second roommate. A warm-hearted Irishman from Boston, he was five foot four, wore a slouch hat, and to me was like a second father. He kept me out of all sorts of trouble. I had several fan clubs, and often in the major cities, groups of teenage girls waited in the lobby hoping to see me come through. Being a star of the show didn't impress Barney at all, and he had a facility for making sure my head size didn't exceed that of my hat. "Jimmie, this is just a job," he would tell me. He warned me that interacting with fans in the lobby after the show could evolve into problems that could get out of hand, so we would always use the back door. He took me with him wherever he went, and I believe his intent was to keep me from hooking up with the wilder members of the cast. Barney was an avid ham radio enthusiast, and nearly every night, he would hang an antenna out of the hotel window and we tuned in to T*he Voice of America,* The *Voice of Moscow,* or *London Calling* to get the latest news of the war. When we played Chicago, he took me out to the Hallicrafter Radio manufacturing headquarters to meet his friend, William Halligan, founder of the company. Hallicrafters was one of the biggest manufacturers of radios in the world. Manufacture of civilian ham radio equipment had been suspended during the war, and the company was designing radios for the military.

We sat across from Halligan's desk and watched with fascination as he proceeded to pour himself a large glass of scotch and milk. He then sat down to talk radios with Barney.

In New York, Boston, and Chicago, Barney would take me to after-hours clubs to hear great jazz musicians including Duke Ellington, Count Basie, and Harry James. I wish I had an opportunity to thank Barney for all the wonderful memories and tell him how much I appreciate all he did for me.

My third roomate was the conductor of our orchestra. He liked to drink and loved women. I recall him rolling in drunk many evenings describing his exploits with various lovelies. One evening he woke me up to tell me about his date that evening. "Jim, she's all heart," he said. I couldn't help but think he'd never taken any courses in anatomy. His stories were always colorful and certainly held my interest.

Bill Provost, a returned veteran, became my fourth roommate. Like most US businesses, Ice Capades guaranteed returning veterans jobs when they came home. Bill had been a line skater and was given his job back when he returned. He certainly didn't resemble any line skater I'd ever seen. He was six foot four and could have easily passed for a linebacker. Bill had served as a Seabee and, when sober, told some hair-raising stories about his war experiences. We didn't room together long. He would get drunk nearly every night but, unlike Leo, would never mention where he had been.

Champions

Bobby Specht, after winning the 1942 US Male Championship, joined Ice Capades. He was one of the most talented people I've ever known. He was one of the skaters who had worked out in St. Paul, so I had often watched him practice. Besides being a fabulous skater, he was, in my opinion, a concert-class pianist. He was handsome and always pleasant to everyone. Girls pursued him relentlessly. He and Donna had been partners, and she was enamored with him. I became Donna's partner when he left for the air force. In the air force, he contracted rheumatic fever and left with a medical discharge. When he recovered, he jumped his contract with Ice Capades and went to skate and dance on the stage with the beautiful Belita. John Harris was furious with his defection and used his influence to make sure they could not get bookings, forcing Bobby to come back and honor his contract with Ice Capades. When he came back to the show, he became one of the first prominent celebrities to "come out" and openly discuss his homosexuality. He stayed involved with Ice Capades for many years.

Aja Zanova had an interesting history. She was born in the late thirties in Czechoslovakia during the reign of the Communists. Close to six feet tall, she was powerfully built. She took up figure skating and eventually became a world champion several times. Following a competition in Canada, she escaped to the West and subsequently was hired by the Ice Follies. She still had a powerful build and was certainly not the female performer ice show audiences were used to seeing. To make matters worse, Ice Follies dressed her in an unflattering American flag costume. Aja lasted one season with Follies and was then cut loose. But she was a survivor. She went to Hollywood, lost a lot of weight, found a choreographer, and became an attractive prospect for an ice show. Ice Capades hired her, and she ended up in Capades International with me.

Denise and Pierre Benoit were a French Canadian pair from Montreal. Their younger sister, Francine, was also with the show and replaced Pierre as Denise's partner after he was called to serve in the Canadian army. They were all very attractive and I was intrigued with their charming accent. Denise married George Eby, who later succeeded

John Harris as president of Ice Capades. Eby, a CPA from Pittsburgh, Pennsylvania, was initially the financial officer with Ice Capades. My favorite memory of Denise and Francine was the night they took me to midnight mass on New Years Eve in Boston.

Robin Lee, five-time US Senior Men's Champion was a classic Nordic, about six one, blond hair, blue eyes, with a husky build. Although Robin was a good performer and had excellent free skating skills, he never seemed to be able to "sell" himself to the audience. After a few years, he left the show entering the ranks of the instructors and then just seemed to fade away.

Nate Walley had been a World Professional Figure Skating Champion. He and his wife, Edith (a former Powers Model), performed for years as a top pair with Ice Capades.

The Unsung

Unsung, but vital to the show, were scores of men and women with particular expertise who traveled with us. Publicists, accountants, choreographers, carpenters, wardrobe specialists and assistants, a company nurse, musicians, and stagehands were also part of "the family."

Norman Frescott was our company manager. His job was to see that the show ran smoothly but also handled the company's travel arrangements, booked hotel rooms, hired local stagehands, and attended to the day-to-day needs of the performers and crew. In addition to having phenomenal problem-solving skills, he was a father figure for the entire company and would listen to personal as well as professional problems members of the company brought to him.

Four railroad boxcars were required to transport the shows props, sets, costumes, and equipment from city to city. Good stagehands were as essential to producing a show as the performers, and they traveled with us on the road to keep us on track and organized. I particularly remember two stagehands from the early days, the Costello brothers. One was short and the other was tall. The short one couldn't read or write, and his brother would have to sign for him when they registered in hotels. They were gregarious and talked constantly.

Setting up the show required a high level of teamwork, and the stagehands and technical crew seemed to work together with the same precision needed in skating routines. They had to set up the complex set, hang the facade, make sure the lighting was set up, and that the props were in the right place at the proper time. Of course, they would dismantle and pack everything up again at the end of the run. The hard work of loading and hauling the costumes, props, and equipment into each arena often had to be done in instances of extreme weather conditions such as blizzards or heat waves.

Brian McDonald, the show's master of ceremonies, was the epitome of a MC, blessed with impressive looks and a mellifluous voice. He was responsible for the sound system. One year he bought a bicycle in Hollywood with the intent to ship it home to Pittsburgh before the show set off for Portland and Seattle. He asked the show's carpenter, Gil Krim, where he might find some wood to build a crate for the bicycle and was told to "look out back" of the arena. Some time later, Gil found McDonald busily sawing and hammering behind the Pan-Pacific arena, but rather than choosing wood from the scrap pile, he had chopped up the Ice Capades bandstand.

Canadian Tours

Ice Capades always played Spokane at Christmas time before setting off on the Canadian tour that began in Victoria, British Columbia, on New Year's Day and finished in late March in Halifax, Nova Scotia. After Victoria, we played Vancouver and then headed over the Canadian Rockies by train for Calgary. One year, avalanches blocked the rail lines to eastern Canada, and the entire show had to be transported by air. When we got off the plane, in Calgary, it was fifty degrees below zero, and the moisture in the air made the sky appear to be filled with sparkling diamonds. In the early days, many of the arenas were small, wooden buildings and such was the case in Calgary. The temperature in the arena was below freezing. To add to the misery, a circus had just played the Calgary arena; backstage, the walkways around the arena were deep in animal urine. Wooden planks were laid down so we could avoid wading through it; however, the planks would bounce as the performers walked over them, and the awful liquid (which due to the salt content did not freeze) would splash onto our bare legs or costumes. We had to wear those costumes every night and could not get them cleaned until we arrived in Edmonton, our next stop. There was no hot water in the dressing rooms, so it was impossible to remove our makeup.

Geographically, to me Canada resembles a great sprawling obese person lying in a chair with a rail line for a belt stretching from Victoria, British Columbia, to Halifax, Nova Scotia. A vast wilderness lies north of the rail lines and the cities. Canada's major cities are on the Canadian Pacific Railroad route from Vancouver, British Columbia, to Winnipeg, Manitoba, and on the Canadian National from Winnipeg to Halifax. As the railroads were built across the country, grand hotels were also constructed in each city to attract visitors. Most were built to resemble European castles and were truly opulent—such as the Banff Springs Hotel near Calgary, the Royal York in Toronto, the Chateau Laurier in Montreal, the Chateau Frontenac in Quebec, and the Lord Nelson in Halifax, Nova Scotia. While on occasion we would stay in one of those grand hotels, we usually stayed in less grand, but still memorable Canadian hotels.

In each city we played, the Company's advanced publicist, Harry Kuh, arranged "publicity calls" for my partner and me to visit radio stations, newsrooms, hospitals, etc. In Edmonton that first year, the call was to visit a children's hospital. We dutifully showed up at the hospital for the publicity photos and were surprised to see children in their beds outside on the veranda in the cold. We were both oblivious to the fact that an epidemic of Tuberculosis was raging among the Inuit and other aboriginal groups in New Foundland and the Northwest Territories at that time. Many had been rounded up and transported to sanitoriums in southern Canada for treatment. Standard treatment in those days consisted of rest and open-air therapy. Exposure to cold pure air was considered so important that it often included having the patient sleep outside. Years later stories were told of how very traumatic the experience had been for those taken as well as those left behind. That memory still tugs at my heart.

In Campbellton, New Brunswick, I recall getting off our company train, bags in hand, and walking from the station to the Hotel Restigouche. The hotel looked like an old, red brick office building with white pillars in front. It was surrounded by snowdrifts well over my head. I loved the sound of the name Restigouche. It is a Mi'kmaq Indian name, which I was told meant, "disobey your elders." That may not be an accurate translation but it is surely the reason I've always remembered that name. The Restigouche River flows nearby and is unique for having one of the largest tidal bores in the world. It was and still is one of the greatest Atlantic Salmon rivers anywhere, with many exclusive fishing lodges owned and operated by wealthy people and corporations. For years, Campbellton had been a destination of many notables who came to fish, hunt, and enjoy its natural wonders. Bing Crosby and Bob Hope used to come to Campbellton for the salmon fishing and stayed at the Restigouche. It is truly a natural paradise; however, for me the Restigouche hotel will always bring to mind the time I was served an apple pie that was strangely flat. When I tried to eat a bite, I found it was very chewy for apple pie. Turns out between the crusts, there were only apple peelings. The rest of the fruit, they explained, was, of course, used for fruit salad.

After the show one evening, I overheard a conversation between two men sitting nearby me in the lobby, who were obviously uncomfortable in their city clothes. They were saying how wonderful it was to be back in civilization. I could only imagine what they'd been up to and where they had come from if they viewed Campbellton as being civilization.

The orchestra we used in Campbellton was not bad for a small village. Most of the members were passable musicians, and they were all volunteer fire fighters. While performing one night, I looked over and noticed that the orchestra leader was waving his baton to an empty orchestra section. There were no musicians, and I was skating to taped music. The entire orchestra had been called away to put out a fire.

The Shark And Two Queens

My third year with the show rolled around, and John Harris invited me to his office, when the show was playing in Pittsburgh. He offered me a new contract and encouraged me to stay with the show, pointing out that should I leave and go to college it would mean a huge loss of income in my peak earning years. My visit with Harris was a mere formality, because my father was the final authority when it came to signing a new contract. I really didn't think Dad would turn down the contract, but he did and at the tour's end I headed back to St. Paul with no idea what was in store for me. While on the road, I'd been given a small portion of my salary as an allowance. The balance was banked, so there was sufficient money to finance my college.

In St. Paul, I found a superb tutor waiting for me. Blois Barrett, a Macalester graduate, was a then graduate student at the University of Minnesota. He was a brilliant student and knew exactly what I needed to do to qualify for college. He tutored me intensively seven days a week for three months. I sat for my high school GED exams and passed. This was the latter part of August in 1946. In September, I sat for entrance exams at Macalester and passed to become an official freshman at

Macalester College. I took a full load, eighteen credits per semester, and went to school year around for three years, intending to do the four-year requirement in three.

One April day in 1949, there was a note on the school bulletin board from John Harris asking that I call him at once. As it had been three years since I'd heard from him and it wasn't time for me to return to the show, I was curious and called him at once. "Jimmy, I'm taking the first American ice show to London. I want you to join the show in Louisville in May. Marshal Alderson will be sending your train tickets."

Somehow, I managed to take my finals early and headed for Louisville. It was Kentucky Derby time, so there was a shortage of hotel rooms and the cast was lodged in Pullman cars. My reentry into the ice show business was not memorable. I was terribly out of shape. Margaret Field was the female lead in the show, and I was paired with her. After the Louisville engagement, we headed for New York City.

As a Minnesota boy, the largest marine vessel I'd ever seen was Ed Pillsbury's forty-foot sailboat on Lake Minnetonka with its Pillsbury blue sails or possibly a paddle-wheeled steamer on the Mississippi River. As I headed down Pier 86 in New York Harbor's *Luxury Row* to board *The Marine Shark*, I got my first glimpse of an ocean-going ship in the distance. *The Marine Shark* was a thirteen thousand ton converted transport ship, which the United States Lines had purchased and converted for passenger use. It was actually small by passenger ship standards, but to me it was enormous and took my breath away. I was apprehensive about the voyage, I must admit. How could anything that big even stay afloat, let alone take me all the way across the Atlantic to South Hampton, England? I was going to be on that monster for five days. Could it weather the fierce Atlantic Storms? Would I be seasick? Fortunately, I was not.

The *Shark's* gun turrets were still in place and attracted a few members of our company who found them to be cozy, secluded spots for romantic interludes. The mess hall was open around the clock, and one evening while having a sandwich, the mess steward revealed to me that the radios in the turrets still operated, and the liaison activity had entertained the ship's crew. All but a few of the cast members were delighted to learn about this.

The trip was fairly calm and the voyage uneventful, and after five days, we finally docked in Southampton. After a short train trip, we arrived in London where we were put up at the Rose Court Hotel near Marble Arch and Hyde Park.

Reservations had been made for us in a modest London hotel near Marble Arch. My London roommate was stilt skater, Gary Johnson, from Laramie, Wyoming. Both of his parents had skated with Sonja Henie's show. To us, six months in London offered an opportunity for a more homelike atmosphere than the usual hotels, so we spent our first few days touring London and looking for apartments.

Gary and I found a luxurious flat in a large apartment complex next to the Thames River called Dolphin Square. The complex must have covered at least two full city blocks. It was five or six stories high, with a large open garden area in the middle. All the conveniences imaginable were available on site, including produce, meat shops, laundromats, dry cleaning, and flower shops. A number of the other cast members lived there also.

Five long years of war had devastated much of London and we were all stunned to see the damage. Block after block had been leveled by the bombing. Around St. Paul's Cathedral, nothing remained but basements for at least a mile in every direction, yet the cathedral was untouched. Rationing was still in effect, and like the English public, we had ration cards. Surviving on them would have been a struggle if friends and relatives had not sent us food parcels to supplement our diets. Bread was in short supply, but for some reason, I was able to get pound cake at the bakery and used to slice it for toast in the morning. Strangely, liquor was not scarce, and our weekend parties were memorable. England's blue laws barred live entertainment on Sundays, so Saturday night was party night. In our first stay in London in 1949, most of us had bicycles and ventured forth to places like Runnymede on the Thames, where the Magna Carta was signed, or Buckingham Palace to watch the changing of the gaurd. We often had picnic lunches alongside the Thames. Often, on the way back to London, our group stopped at pubs along the way for a beer or two. After a few stops, some had to get a cab to take themselves and their bikes back home.

Our grand opening at the eight-thousand-seat Empress Hall in Earl's Court, London, was a much-heralded event. John Harris was there and, as special added attractions, brought along Donna Atwood and Markus and Thomas. Many of London's elite came to the show, including members of the British royal family. Arab royalty were also present at rink side with servants preparing food from braziers during our performance. Following the show, the company manager came to my dressing room and told me that I was invited to a reception. I went upstairs to a packed reception room. Several of the other performers were there when I arrived. The tables were filled with finger food, and drinks were flowing freely. Food was still scarce and rationed in London in 1949, so the display of this much food was rare. I was being introduced to the building manager, Sir Claude Langdon, when a tall, distinguished man in the center of the room caught my attention. His identity was unmistakable. It was the Duke of Edinburgh, and beside him stood a short well-dressed woman about my age. It was Princess Margaret. Sir Claude introduced me to both of them, and Princess Margaret and I struck it off immediately. She came to the show several times and seemed to always make sure to say hello to me. Sometimes I wondered what might have progressed if she had not been a royal.

A routine element of Howard (Sully) Sullivan's comedy act was to kiss a bald-headed man in the front row. Management pointed out a certain man for Sully to target and that man turned out to be the Prime Minister of England, Clement Attlee. It became an international incident, and of course, management denied having put Sully up to committing such an offense.

After a six-month engagement at Empress Hall, we headed for South Hampton and boarded the *Marine Shark* for home. We didn't learn until we arrived in New York that it was the *Shark*'s last voyage, nor did we know some of its steel plates had been cracking dangerously as we headed for New York. I later learned the *Shark's* postwar history included returning US Corregidor and Bataan prisoners of war to San Francisco, transporting European holocaust survivors, and repatriating Americans to the United States. Repatriation was still taking place all over the world, even four years after the war. On our trip to London, along with our cast of over one hundred, two hundred German passengers had been aboard and were on their way home to be repatriated.

The following spring I was again walking down a New York pier to board a ship bound for England. This time, however, it was the forty-three thousand ton *Queen Elizabeth*, at that time, the largest passenger ship ever built. She began her service as a troopship in 1940 and, after the war, was refurbished and refitted into what was described as a floating palace. The *Marine Shark* had one class of passenger service and was quite stark, but the *Queen* was luxurious, with grand spiral staircases, luscious food, exotic drinks, and assigned seating for meals. Alas, there were no gun turrets!

The *Queen Elizabeth* made it to South Hampton in just under four days compared to the *Shark's* five. However, on the evening of the third day, a ferocious Atlantic storm occurred. It was truly a "dark and stormy night." The waves swept over the bow, totally enveloping the huge ship, which plowed steadily forward. Fortunately, the *Queen* had stabilizers that prevented her from rolling from side to side as lesser ships might do. When we arrived in South Hampton, I noticed the four-inch steel plates on the bridge had been mangled like pretzels, attesting to the power of the mighty gale.

This year, I rented a nice apartment in London in Chelsea, again on the Thames, and this time I lived alone. My favorite feature of this apartment was the marvelous library in the apartment that contained first editions of Dickens stories.

It was a heady time for all of us, and as the weeks went by, I began to develop an attraction for my partner that resulted in marriage the following December. The marriage lasted for fourteen years and ended in 1963. The high point of the marriage was the births of our two wonderful children—Jamie and Kathy. Both are a joy and a source of pride.

We again performed for six months at Empress Hall in Earl's Court and headed for home. This time we sailed on the *Queen Mary*, an older version of the *Queen Elizabeth*. As we were preparing to depart, I was standing by the rail watching the passengers board. A man with reddish hair, wearing a full-length black leather German army SS greatcoat came aboard. I later learned the stranger was Edi Rada, the prewar European figure skating champion who had won the European Men's bronze medal in 1939, the last World Championship before the war. The previous year, 1949, the first Championships after the war were held in Paris, and Edi was the bronze medal winner. He would be joining our show. None of us ever saw him on the ship during the voyage.

Edi's premiere performance in the United States was in Johnstown, Pennsylvania. It was a big media event, and all the top Capades brass were present. Rada was introduced with great fanfare. The curtains parted, and he stepped through them and fell flat on his face. To make matters worse, it was as if he was attempting to skate on ball bearings. He could not even stand up. It was a disaster. Someone had put scotch tape on the bottom of his blades, and without edges, it is impossible to stand up on skates. We eventually learned the culprit was a comedian, Willie Kall. As time went on, hostilities evaporated, and everyone accepted Edi.

In the middle of the Irish Sea, we had another storm, not on the magnitude of the *Elizabeth* storm, but a storm it was. The next morning was calm and clear. However, I realized we were dead in the water with two large black balls hoisted on the mast. I thought that was hilarious and asked a passing officer what the balls meant. He told me it was a warning to other ships to stay clear because we were out of control. It seems a rudder chain had broken during the night.

Somber Memories

DONNA   JAMIE
ATWOOD   LAWRENCE
              stars of the
famous "Ice Capades of 1944" playing
at Maple Leaf Gardens this week
          Sold you your
WAR SAVINGS STAMPS TODAY

Wednesday, December 8, 1943
WVS War Savings Stamp Booth at Simpson's

10. Donna and Jim War Bond Promotion

World War II was not waged by the military alone. During World War II, the war was foremost in the thoughts of all Americans. There was hardly a family without close friends or family members in the service. Each city and town in America had block wardens to make sure no lights were showing during an air raid. The nations speed limit was 35 mph and driving was limited to essential travel. Butter, cheese, meat, coffee, and suger were among the many things rationed and everyone looked for scrap metal to turn in. Even toothpaste tubes, foil from cigarette packages and bacon grease were valued as raw material.

Keeping up public morale on the home front was vital to the war effort, and most of the top film stars, sports heroes, and other celebrities volunteered much of their time for personal appearances and special entertainment events for the troops. It was said that entertainment was the only commodity that wasn't rationed. By the end of 1943, Ice Capades had entertained over one hundred thousand service men and women. Sales of war bonds were needed to fund the war, and the War Department set a goal to sell one billion dollars a month. Donna and I made appearances at war bond rallies in every town we played. Ice Capades received an award from the government for selling seventeen million dollars worth of war bonds in 1943.

At the time, the draft board took nearly any male who could walk. With so many men making sacrifices for the country, I often felt guilty that I wasn't one of them. Shortly after my eighteenth birthday, I flew home to St. Paul and reported to the induction center for my physical. I had every reason to believe they would take me. Our forces were engaged in horrific battles with the Japanese in the South Pacific, and things were not going well. When I got to the first exam table, the doctor took one look at my history, and when he read that I was asthmatic, he told me to put on my clothes and leave. I couldn't believe it. A second time, I was told to report to the recruiting center, this time in the Watts area in Los Angeles. We were playing at the Pan Pacific Arena in Hollywood. Again, I was sure I would be recruited, and my employers were too. The process repeated itself. I got to the first table and was told to leave.

As veterans began to return from the war, the company often had special performances for them. Reactions to the show were always quite different from those of civilian audiences. The First Marine Division fought the first major offensive by allied troops in the Pacific theater at Guadalcanal. After seven months of intense fighting both the Japanese and tropical diseases, they forced the Japanese to evacuate the island. It was a horrendous battle and our first victory in the war against the Japanese in the Pacific. The division went on to fight in New Guinea, Tarawa, Peleliu, Tinian, Saipan, and Okinawa, some of the bloodiest battles of the war. When they returned to the United States, they were taken to a hospital near Philadelphia, Pennsylvania. We were playing in Philadelphia at the time, and a special performance was arranged for them. They had not been on the US mainland in three years and had hardly seen a female during that time. The arena seated six thousand, and was filled with these brave men who had fought so long and so hard. During each show, we had come to know where we could likely expect a reaction from the crowd. During the entire hour and a half of that show, however, there was almost no reaction or applause, just a bit of laughter for some of the comics. It was eerie. Virginia married a first lieutenant from that First Marine Division about three months after that performance. I never learned how they connected.

Another unforgetable memory for me was a benefit we did in the Maple Leaf Gardens in Toronto for Canadian veterans. The front row was occupied with men not much older than me. Most were missing arms or legs, a couple were quadriplegic and some were on stretchers. It seemed strange to be flying around out there in my prime without a care in the world before young men, who had sacrificed so much in service to their country. It was a sobering experience for all of us.

The Magic of Music

As you watch a dancer or skater perform, do you ever considered the elements that make up the performance? Things that must be considered for each number in an ice show performance include: where the person appears in the show's running order, what act precedes him or her, which act follows, the type and quality of the costume. All these are important, but the most important factor to an act is the music. Is it appropriate to the particular skills and technique of the performer? Is the audience familiar with the music? Does it move the audience? As you watch a performance, you may not be aware of it, but these elements are all operating.

The size and quality of the orchestra make a big difference to the performer. Each arena had "house minimums," the minimum number of musicians required in that arena. Most cities had a minimum of eighteen. Our show carried a lead trumpet, pianist, drummer, the leader, and his assistant. The quality of the locals varied a lot. In Hollywood, we had studio musicians who were outstanding, as were the BBC musicians when we played in London. The minimum in Toronto was fifty. Having a big band was an incredible delight.

The local unions would supplement our musicians when we were on the road. Occasionally, we were lucky to be joined by a musician who was a star in his or her own right. When this happened, our orchestra leader encouraged the musician to improvise. Several times when we performed in New Orleans, the famous trumpet player, Al Hirt, played with us. I don't know why he did this. It certainly wasn't for the money because he performed with us as a union musician, at union wages. He seemed to love playing with us and would sit on the edge of the bandstand and blow his heart out.

Few performers were given a choice in the selection of their music, and in some cases, especially to this neophyte, that was a blessing. Skating to selections from *American in Paris, Student Prince,* and *Brigadoon* were choices far beyond my scope at the time, but each certainly enhanced my career.

It wasn't long before hearing an appealing music selection would turn my mind to skating, and I could easily do the choreography for a solo or pair in my mind. I still do that to this day.

Two of the show's orchestra leaders will always be memorable to me. Jerry Mayhall was the leader when I first joined the show and had been with the Ice Capades since its inception. His hobby was photography. He took me under his wing, and soon, I had several state of the art cameras and went on photo outings with him in each city. I collected over three hundred flower pictures and had an offer from a calendar company to use some of my flower pictures for one of their calendars.

Leo Strini, the orchestra leader for Ice Capades West, was very talented, and I always appreciated his excellent musicianship, his vitality, and his friendship.

In each city, the leader rehearsed with the local musicians. The amount of time dedicated to each performer's music was critical to the success of the performance. It is a key element in how you connect with the audience. The soloist described in a previous chapter as "all heart" figured this out immediately and decided to be sure that she was number one with the orchestra leader. She was skilled in the ways of the world and her music was always the best in the show. I couldn't begin to compete with her, and I knew it. My music was okay but never quite as inspired as hers.

Not So Smooth

Striving for perfection, you are still subject to the unexpected. During the era of the American ice show, the major shows toured forty-four weeks a year. One year, while playing in the Midwest, a guy showed up and hung around backstage for about a week. When we'd come off the ice, he'd take our pulse and temperature. We later learned he was a professor from the University of Michigan conducting a study to determine how much energy a professional figure skater expended in a four-minute solo or pair. The study found the energy expended was equivalent to that of an average worker in an eight-hour day. When you consider we toured forty-four weeks a year and did anywhere from nine to eleven shows a week, that was a striking piece of information. Multiply forty-four times anywhere from nine to eleven shows a week, and you have an opportunity to have all sorts of things happen that are not a part of the routines. Performers may have a special talent, but beneath the glitzy costumes, they are mere humans. Although they are performing for the audience, sometimes they're thinking about the party or meal after the show or whether they've got a phone call from someone special waiting when they get back to the hotel.

Mishap in New Brunswick

The condition of the ice is critical to performance. It must be hard to reduce the friction of the blades and permit speed, but not so hard that the skater cannot "take an edge." For ice shows, the manufacture of ice is a multistage process of layering ice and paint. If the ice covering the paint layer is not thick enough, it can cause a skate to catch and stop the skater abruptly. One opening night in St. Johns, New Brunswick, I was carrying Gini Baxter down the ice in an overhead lift. I hit a bare spot on the ice and fell flat on my face, launching Gini into the front row. By some miracle, no one was hurt.

Bad Timing

Performing under the spotlights on the ice, you can usually only make out faces in the first five or six rows. If I noticed a particularly attractive woman in the front row, I would sometimes flirt within the bounds of what I thought I could get away with. Usually, I would get a reaction, and that added a dimension to the performance.

One evening in performance at the Forum in Montreal, I noticed several lovely ladies seated stage left in the front row. I decided to give them a little special attention the next time I skated past them. The set for the show was one hundred feet across by thirty feet deep. Metal framing twelve feet high supported it all. Our eighteen to twenty-five piece orchestra was on top, and the front portrayed our theme. That year, we had a patriotic theme, and the set featured an elegant American eagle. The wings were moved forward so the skaters could enter or exit the ice from both the right and left side. The middle was the head of a large bald eagle.

John Harris, owner of the show, would occasionally come to town unannounced, buy a ticket, and sit in the audience to assess their reaction to the show. As I was about to impress the women with a flying pass, I spotted him sitting right next to them. Seeing him unnerved me, and I crashed right into one of the eagle's wings at about thirty miles an hour. Fortunately, the wing was heavily padded, and I bounced off undamaged. Harris never mentioned the incident to me.

11. Jimmy the Big Leap

Bad Timing - Again

London did not allow live entertainment on Sundays, so during our six-month
stay, a group of us, occasionally, chartered a plane for the thirty-minute flight

to Paris, where we would stay up around the clock for great food and clubs, especially the famous Lido Club where I first saw totally nude dancers. Then we'd fly back to London Monday afternoon for the evening show. One Monday evening I had a rude shock. I was sure that despite overindulging in rich food and having been up all night, I was performing just fine. I normally finished my number in front of the set with my trademark crossfoot spin. This particular Monday evening, I finished my crossfoot only to discover I was at the wrong end of the ice. And once again, John Harris just happened to be sitting in the front row smiling and slowly clapping.

Giggles and Bladders and Ducks - Oh No!

Shoot the Duck is a skating move in which the skater crouches down on one leg as far as possible and glides on one foot, while holding the other foot straight out in front. It's often used in line numbers. One night during a chorus number, something struck the girls as funny, and they were stifling giggles for most of the number. When the time came to move into Shoot the Duck position, the girl at the head of the line could no longer control both the giggles and her bladder, and a yellow stream began to trail the ice behind the group. Unfortunately that mishap earned her the nickname, "P.P.," which she endured as long as she was with the show.

A Letdown

All the ice shows had excellent costume departments, staffed by expert costume designers who knew how to make costumes that not only looked good but that would not inhibit the skater's ability to perform. That is no small task. Only on rare occasions would failures occur. One evening Donna and I were in the middle of a number at Madison Square Garden. She was wearing a one shoulder strap costume top, and that strap gave way and the top of her costume fell off. The lighting director quickly killed the lights, and I helped her off the ice.

The Show Must Go on

Nearing the weekend of another successful run in Chicago, I began experiencing a sore throat along with some swelling that I ignored. On the train to our next engagement in St. Louis, my condition worsened, and by the time we arrived in St. Louis, I wasn't feeling well at all and told the company manager, Norman Frescott. He called a doctor, who examined me in my hotel room and diagnosed me as having the mumps. He told Frescott he might have to quarantine the entire cast. Friends suddenly appeared and packed my bags. Before I knew it, I was being smuggled out of the hotel and onto a train bound for St. Paul. No one ever found out, and the show did go on. I missed the engagements in St. Louis and Fort Worth and then rejoined the show for the opening in Hollywood. Fortunately, none of the other performers came down with the mumps.

Casting for Gold

Bill Dennis was the drummer with Ice Capades International, but Bill did not look like your average drummer. He was six two, had shoulders like a linebacker, and black curly hair, and I never saw him without a smile. He could dance like a ten year old and often did. Besides being a superb show drummer, he was a genuine war hero. During the Second World War, he was in the thick of the "Battle of The Bulge," one of the bloodiest battles of the war. During that terrible siege, he was relieving himself in the forest when a German 88 antitank shell went right between his legs. He survived without a scratch or the need to change his position in the choir.

Bill married Marge McMillan, a skater in the line. Marge and her brother Ian came from Canada, and both skated in the chorus. They were the offspring of the family that founded and owned British Sino Limited—genuine Hong Kong Tai Pans with the big office building in Hong Kong. British Sino made and sold everything from trains to jade. One Christmas Bill's mother-in-law sent him a gorgeous teak box about two feet long with intricate carvings, which contained a beautiful, split bamboo fly rod in sections with several hand-tied flies. He was an avid fly fisher and was taken by the present. He learned it was a handmade product from China and could be bought for next to nothing. He surmised that American fly fishermen would sacrifice their youngest child to get their hands on one of these beauties.

A few days after he had developed a sales plan, he called me and suggested that I become his partner in a venture to sell them. We had a perfect set up to do this. We were about to tour across Canada, starting in Victoria, and playing all the Canadian cities until we reached Halifax, Nova Scotia, in the spring. I put up my share; we bought a large supply of handmade fly rods and started to sell to sporting goods stores in each city we played. They sold like hot cakes; we had a hard time meeting the demand. Shortly before we reached Halifax, Bill and I began to get phone calls from sporting goods stores wanting their money back. It seems that when these marvelous fly rods got wet, the glue that held the split bamboo together failed. By the time the dust settled, our venture that looked so promising had cost us both a bundle. It seemed like such a good idea at the time.

Making The Break

Dressing room conversation among the older men of our cast centered mostly around past glories and how much they were valued in the "old days." This prompted a determination in me to quit while still at the top. Thanks to my father's insistence, as the only college-educated person in the dressing room, I had options that the others lacked. I was ready to take advantage of my education and move on to explore other challenges and opportunities.

People in the entertainment business are almost never able to celebrate the holidays. Christmas, Thanksgiving, and New Years simply mean that you are going to do extra shows, sometimes three shows on New Years Day. So while I enjoyed my job, the prospect of being home instead of on the road for months at a time was appealing.

By then, Margaret and I had two children. They were well cared for and content in the show environment, but they were missing the opportunity to interact with other children and participate in normal childhood activities. In 1956 we left the show and began a new life.

Seven years after later, John Harris sold Ice Capades for $5 million to Metromedia. He'd seen the show through twenty-three successful years, and it was still going strong. Dick Palmer, who had been with Ice Capades since the early days, managed the show for Metromedia. Dick was a great innovator and possessed an intimate knowledge of the business and technical workings of the show. Under his management, the show continued to be successful. But the ice show business was changing, and Metromedia sold the show in 1986. Several more sales followed, but subsequent owners could not find the right formula to adapt to societal changes. The not-so-grand finale for the great show came in 1995 when it closed down forever.

Ice Follies merged with Holiday on Ice in 1979 and is now produced on a much smaller scale by an Amsterdam, Netherlands, company.

The contemporary American touring shows have a lot of appeal. Tom Collins, Scott Hamilton, and others have done a superb job of maintaining some semblance of performing theater on ice. However, today's ice shows consist of a relatively small collection of world-famous champions, each doing his or her routine to recorded music. They have the finest skaters, state-of-the-art sound systems, remarkable lighting effects, and a few excellent novelty acts. But they are essentially exhibitions with nice bells and whistles and rely on recruiting the most recent world and Olympic champions to attract an audience.

Gone are the fabulous production numbers featuring large precision chorus lines, with elaborate costumes and headdresses. Also gone are the orchestras playing live music and, alas, the XK120 Jaguars.

The era of the marvelous touring extravaganzas is over. Looking back on those golden days, I marvel at the way the elements came together and made it possible for them to flourish, and I'm grateful that I had the opportunity to play a small part in the wondrous phenomenon that was the great American touring ice show.

Farewell Ice Capades

When he decided to leave the show, the great English pair skater and teacher, Robert Dench wrote this poem and gave it to me. He has been gone for some time now, but if he were here, I hope he would be pleased with this modest attempt to "have these troubles understood."

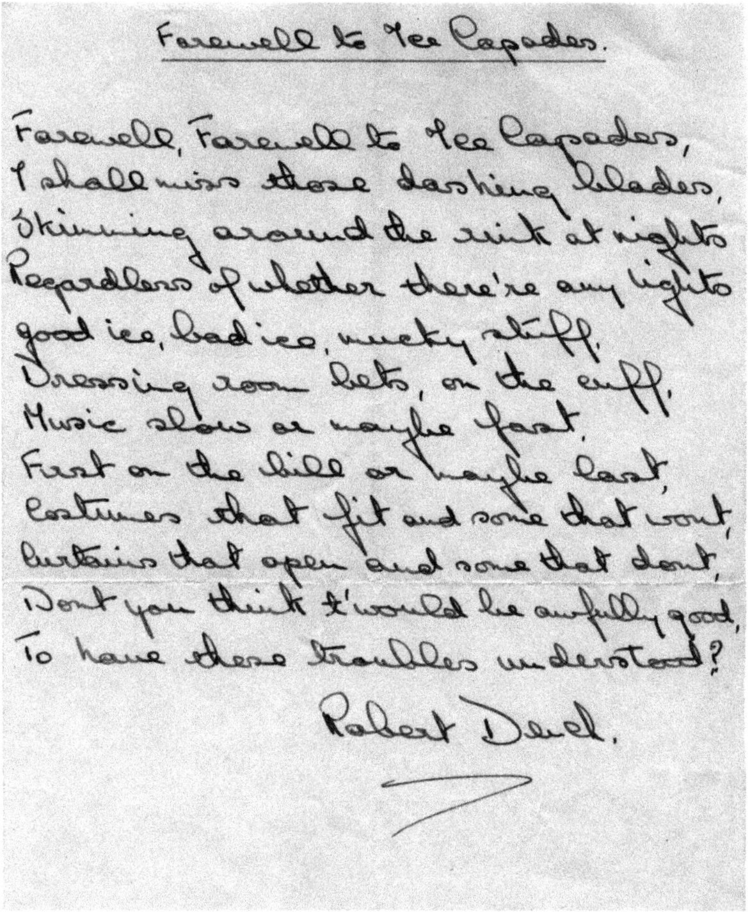

Farewell to Ice Capades.

Farewell, Farewell to Ice Capades,
I shall miss those dashing blades,
Skimming around the rink at nights
Regardless of whether there're any lights
good ice, bad ice, mucky stuff,
Dressing room bets, on the cuff,
Music slow or maybe fast,
First on the bill or maybe last,
Costumes that fit and some that wont,
Curtains that open and some that dont,
Dont you think t'would be awfully good,
To have these troubles understood?

Robert Dench.

12. Robert Dench Poem

CPSIA information can be obtained
at www.ICGtesting.com
Printed in the USA
LVHW081559060421
683586LV00017B/1685

9 780615 643373